You've Just Been Told

Also by Elizabeth Macklin

A Woman Kneeling in the Big City

You've Just Been Told

P O E M S

Elizabeth Macklin

W. W. Norton & Company

New York   London

For information about permission to reproduce selections from this
book, write to Permissions, W. W. Norton & Company, Inc.,
500 Fifth Avenue, New York, NY 10110

The text of this book is composed in Slimbach Book
with the display set in Seagull Light
Composition by PennSet, Inc.
Manufacturing by The Courier Companies, Inc.
Book design by Charlotte Staub

Library of Congress Cataloging-in-Publication Data

Macklin, Elizabeth.
     You've just been told / Elizabeth Macklin.
        p. cm.
     ISBN 0-393-04867-5
       I. Title.

     PS3563.A318737 Y68 2000
     813'.54—dc21   99-059714

W. W. Norton & Company, Inc., 500 Fifth Avenue, New York,
N.Y. 10110
www.wwnorton.com

W. W. Norton & Company Ltd., 10 Coptic Street, London WC1A 1PU

1 2 3 4 5 6 7 8 9 0

For Mary Painter

Contents

Grammars of attention

In Galilea I Listen

1

Half the house here belongs to me. Half belongs to sound.
Rain on roof tiles remade the old wooden xylophone.
An echo chain on a well bucket—was that known?

And don't tell me that's a usual blue—that stucco wall,
yellows breaking the heat before it, beside
a bougainvillea.

But noontime bees are loud as sirens,
the wind is loud as trucks.
I could be at home.

2

The light last night from the candle-kitchen made a cube
of white in the mist outside—an anteroom
of light on the sandstone.

And where is the past tense for all these pictures?
Far away. No gradual spectrum leads you here.
You go from white through a door

into all the colors: A ship standing out
in the distant sky—copper
in a blue-green harbor.

3

Home is not home without a colored harbor in it
(I sang). Zinc-gray shingles or siding
will not do now.

What I find hard to hear is what I've been
glad to leave: what it's been like
back there

for who's been left—the nonexistent crystal weather
in a flat township, its "I shan't mind,
shall you?"

4

Sometimes a day is a blueprint meadow: esparto spread to dry
in a center sun—red-clay pitchers in shade
on the edge. Today was one.

Sheep move around concealed in a thicket corner. Bells
ring clank inside the oak trees. Bordering poppies
mortar the morning taut in a cool breeze.

Today the burning fields made an old song: girls sang
"Shepherdess Walk" to a fire, as if their love were
sure to arrive, a godhouse escaped to a godtown.

Cast-Aluminum Espresso Pot

Where one mother cleaned the pot,
scrubbing and boiling
the thing in ammonia finally, one did not.

One left a light film of coffee on,
as much as would not
come off with water alone, and some rubbing.

So? What harm would it do?
The pot grew brown over
time: it showed how a flame threw

heat in a black design from a blue burner
over the years, and how you, too,
could get away with not having everything silver.

Imagine

Once I spoke a foreign language
in a dream—like skating, like swimming in air.
Like flying:
I was able to reach
the doctor, was able to save
the loved one, able to make myself

understood. The looks askance,
the dumb stares,
were nods and smiles:
agreement.
A white-coat bureaucrat turned
obliging, allowed me into intensive care

to be with the loved one, who was dying.
I spoke the most foreign language.
I loved, I hoped,
I dreamed
that I said the needful thing.
Bien morir, or There, there.

Or Here. I could say everything.
No, I could speak
no foreign language.
I was not able.
Not having done a thing, except in a dream.
I was not there.

A Myth for the Girl at Bedtime

For my mother, Margaret Herkenratt Wood

What was not spoken so hope could grow: Her father disappearing, or not. The long, slow half-heard fight in the long evening or long morning. The beets eaten up each night—a little joke. The "Get out"—untold—"and earn money." Life faraway, as a song, because required. Not telling her fears as fear: how a mystery, somehow managed, like crowns for molars, a filling, a married life.

Her hopes for the new property: its raspberries, water, field—its charmed setting, woods, water, a field, "like the farm." Other truths unspoken aloud till later: "I had such hopes for that place, but I couldn't do it alone." A bad part of speech: How the beautiful noun changes meaning over the years—a picture still being developed; its haze still clear. How the discouraged rhyme keeps watch over its little girl: Disappointments caught in the act of meeting, trying or not to be healed. Though longing. And telling a story that's true:

Somebody's raising a curtain on Hope and Beauty—a mother and her mother—long abandoned: in sandals, skirts, in hats. A scatter of music anyhow, in corners—"Damn'd if you don't, damn'd if you do"—to tell a listener they're in fact alive. Hope speaks haltingly out loud—the reason for doubt. Beauty paints golden patterns on her china, on the background, plays the broken piano, urges her daughter to harmonize.

You've Just Been Told

to move to
Wolfe Island:

a rounded island in a wide
river at the edge of a wide, dark lake.

You've just been told
to move to Wolfe Island. What

will you find there?
Wolves?

Traps for wolves?
You've

been told to move to Wolfe Island.
What can you take along when you go?

All the kitchenware.
All the hammers and saws.

This book and that book.
Whatever your choice was.

You'll take a free ferry
to Wolfe Island. The car

has its brakes set and won't roll.
The ferry clanked into the dock

of the island.
What do you find there?

A small town. A red stop sign.
Islands of squared-off fields

in a pond of trees.
Little-box houses in square

yards. Clouds spread over the trees,
as flat as icing. Fences,

green wheat. A second shore.
A road with a name like

Button Edge Road?
Can't we go back and look?

Later. Don't worry.
Now we live here.

The Homeland

What are your principal products? How
can I memorize you? Stone fruits grown by heart.
Or grain—bread—or Guernsey cattle. I need ships to know you.

These three have been your woods—worked out
in the mother tongue: Ironwood bent to be ships. Flowering
home-carved cherry heartwood. Bark—birch—for a dead-bell drum.

Finally land and see the tower of her dreams: it's tall,
white, with a world tilting on the top part—
a spade balanced on the world. It's where she falls from.

What I Said Afterward

Used to be I could lie like crazy—lie
to you, to "save my life," lie
to be "pretty"—and not know it.

Leaves underneath were green
with light in moments of—
call it horror. A dahlia might
spread creased magenta petals—
intricate, showy—when the time came

to be lonely. Used to be
I could hold off—wait—wait
to tell the truth. Now there isn't any.

June Intercedes in the Garden of Roses

There is no hurry—no hurry today.
No one you love is going to die.

The huddled gold roses. The showy pink ones, bright-
pink, under a mackerel sky.

Was it irrevocable loss that kept you awake
last night? Fear of irrevocable loss?

The huddled gold roses, the showy pink ones bright-
white. Like

her mother's letters, in plain writing,
in their envelopes, that she saved:

those were the things that made
her cry.

That grief has now been placed
at a remove.

But the rose that's queen of the May, the June, July,
was already planted by human hands. It can contain

this. No church, no figure of speech, can make you love
actual loss.

The peach-down roses, splayed single-petals wavery, fragrant,
near white.

Was it the fear of loss
that kept you awake last night?

There's no hurry, no hurry, today.
No one you love is going to die.

1,985 Years Through a Word Between Us

A.D. 8–1993

Of course Ovid wrote *Relapsa est*
when she slipped back,

climbing the hill, the Roman road
away from death.

Orpheus knew at first to dream her,
sing her, pray her, while walking,

to follow: non-Greek words
to mimic the rising line

of a music, the notes unceasing,
to be triumphant.

But Ovid wrote down *Relapsa est*,
and we have our under-

standing: exhaustion greater
and greater and doubt as

gravity pulls effluvium
into the heart

to break up the tacit promise
and make us doubt.

As, to try to escape to gravity, water
sluices down channels to

roses in stone and lotus,
just like Eurydice,

though she relapsed
through a failure,

a word slipped sidewise, into the medicine,
aural but visible late mnemonic:

Orpheus turned and stopped
singing. *Relapsa est.*

A Chance Small Fruit

In the taste
of this sour apple
is the bee
making pictures
of honey. First
there's a branch
toward the middle of a
not-tall tree. Then a bud
and a not-pink, not-
white flower—a cup
for itself, the bee.
Then a hard green
apple-thumb is round
and redder. Success!
But still green.
I come eat it. I miss
my place on the tree.
I miss the sun
on my hand.
I miss the tree.

The Imaginary Picnic

In me still, she takes me fishing for tadpoles,
down the long hill to the pond. Has found the hole
where the book slid behind the baseboard.
Says the light-indigo flowers on the bank are *laurel*.

Today I light my cigarette from her brother's,
my uncle's. Later I give him mine to light his from,
sheltered from the wind the boat has made.
You see why we do all this. Or you see some.

You my immediate reader, next of kin,
all too similar underneath—you cannot win
in comparison with that day / this day.
It is too green. The food, its lifelong taste, paintable,

on this picnic table. I had a mother who loved me.
Our sky is *blue* behind lit leaves on the family tree:
too easy an explanation. But our trip down to the water
was not / is not a "conspiracy."

Now come the cousins' children, bringing their visual machines:
their dog and their cat near-wild and needing training.
They've done this so the day will be
easier to remember. My mother sings her desire in me,

recasting unescaped need. I told her,
It can happen by accident—not what I mean.
It has happened, I would say. *It is not your "fault."*
I am glad it has happened to me.

Fall Back

N.Y.; S.F.

On a day like this, when I have no paper
and look for scraps, the sun sets early.
It's black at five. My grandmother, too, surely
had days like this, even when she was young.
She was a bitter woman.

I've been to the market, some days before
a day like this, and bought food,
bought fruit. I make sure to buy, too, some
one thing I haven't seen in an age.
Today, in October, it's sumac.

They don't wear gloves nowadays
to go downtown. No change in dress,
I think, on a day like this, could change
my uninherited nature: I chose this; I know
how I look in pictures.

In summer it would be light now.
The slit courtyards allowing the light,
I'd have a hardened field of sky, trampled
by clouds. Even on a day like this,
I'd have my small certainty.

I'm not hungry or thirsty today. I can read
long words from far away, in place and time,
and understand them; turn on a light
when it's five. My grandmother, too, often had
days like this, but she was a bitter woman.

Foolishly Halved, I See You

The white-green wheel of a sliced lime
after a day: so naturally dry,

and so protective of all its remaining
juice. This is the quick thought so sly
of the classic survivor. But you have survived

the living! the only in doubt,
for now, the only in danger.

Now the foolish attempt to—*wait*—not think
about the cut fruit. No, don't cry,

not yet, over its unspilled half-green
milk. It dries hard overnight. I
am you. And the dying hasn't died

yet. In fact, is perhaps not dying,
although—you do too love him—he is in danger.

Almost

A qualifier of superlatives

How much of this
was misunderstanding—
how much was almost blindness?
We did math at the table

almost forever. Or I "helped"
around your finicking chores.
I almost certainly thought
you couldn't see me.

You almost always said
yet again *"You with me?"*
I was certainly
angry with you.

Dear Old Dad (your almost ironical
nickname; your invention), explain
our delay in getting the gist
of kindness. I didn't see you almost

might've but couldn't;
you didn't tell me stories
about your childhood.
You were maybe afraid, almost.

And so, almost maybe, was I.
But beatings, chiggers in Texas,
butter borrowed on welfare
are almost laughable

after a lifetime,
fears of a blank
or angry passion
almost a memory.

Wholly unique (though yes we
have no degrees of uniqueness)
your almost irreconcilable
lifetime:

qualifying the present
and almost the past
by strict, strong, stronger
grammars of attention—

just when you're thinking
of dying, you marry again,
quickly, almost ecstatic,
trusting at last your almost

perfect decision, your superlative.
Yet almost just as jealous
of each wife, child/children:
how our love is apportioned.

See? I'm almost
with you again.
I'm almost angry
with you again.

Yet Another Categorical Imperative

After my grandmother Adelaide Siegert Wood

It was an unsuccessful escape. Thus
the sight of a "brooch," a "broach"—a pin
passed on but sold at a yard sale.
Not stolen. Nothing at all to see
or be mean about: all of the handmade dolls
had been and gone, into a vacuum; not been saved
as mementos of a particular woman.

She'd made dolls, dressed and embroidered
father and mother and baby. She had preened them,
pretended to play, made up a different family.
She was overinsistent; silent. Liked to be pleased
to act out of charity. She sat and entertained
groundless suspicions. She made herself unpleasant.
She invisibly loved her immediate offspring.

She couldn't contain herself; she didn't.
She called him *just like your old man!*, crying,
stole back the old ring—gold, ruby, heavy,
shaped like a dragon. She crooned over brooches,
little dresses: *"Schöne! Wie geht's?"* She sat
and she made more dolls. She wanted them saved.
She plainly wanted somebody to love her.

It was an unhappy escape—trains
back and forth and back from San Francisco.
She died without thinking. She was afraid,
I'm sure. She had been sick, been crying;
she'd harbored the same suspicions. She died without
telling her son "I love you"; died without thinking,
half believing. She didn't succeed in time.

Psalm 103 & Vanity

"The LORD is full of compassion
and mercy, long suffering
and of great goodness."
Why aren't YOU?

The littlest thing overthrows you
into bad feeling in the
worst way. In THE worst way,
or one of them,

as in a dream
a black-brown cancer became
a 3-inch block, without *your*
having noticed, until too late.

Why won't you take steps to guard
the lightness of heart
that comes from trying to SEE straight;
or to make amends, even late.

The railroad bridges' stone
is ALLOWED to be overgrown.
Is clearing away the ivy
(maintenance!) vanity?

The Secret Note You Were Handed by Lorca

It's a song: *dormida, sleeping*. You're asleep,
and not only "drowsy." The way a true friend
returns after dying, *penando*, the old dog lost
but returning to leap and to love you: a dream,

not only a daydream, thinking the words
with leashed feelings.

Was it truly different for you: sun scorned—lost
in a stolen shadow, as if for a stolen girl,
as if in an envy? He, too, nearly assumed
you'd been longing for something different.

A friend comes back in a dream,
it's funny—the same jacket,

the tied yellow tie but the same gesture.
And the marvelling wash of the old
affection, humming—a blue-gold snow in between,
like a sun indoors over coolness.

If only—
It's only a dream.
Was it you that hurt him?

See. See?

See where the frog
under the grass bank sits—
Where I would sit
if I were afraid.

I came down to the lake
this morning, to get away
from the dish/spoon clash
of familiar, familial

loving. Frog sits
rocking on the round
chest of his breathing.
I've seen his black-and-green

eye, I've seen the light
make a wet spot in it.
And there's the tight gold
line of his underjaw,

there's his small large body.
The question: *Why don't you
want to catch him?* A new
answer: *Because he's scared.*

Out in the wet cool air, this
frog's cheeks shudder
like gills out of water.
And I am not yet perfect,

either. I am not yet
adult and whole. I didn't
keep myself from moving. Too green.
He had to leap.

The Sadness of Not Knowing

Two years to the minute
    (where *was* I?) when
she was alone, the nurse left, and she

was alone—strong, weakened,
    living in hope or
icebound or white-sheet lonely?

I was getting my tickets when this
    last minute, last hour
took place. Yes, I see

    how it was.
I hope there *was* a heaven.

"Oh, *nonsense*," she'd say to the fear
    in the thought, she
might have said.

"Don't be afraid.
    Don't be afraid
to be sad,

to be there, away, to try
    to see."

Grief Like a Physicist Finding
the Quantum of Action

He's "arbitrarily" given the moment a number,
called a *constant*. Consigned all the fading light
to a *particle, wave*, to *all it looks like.*

He missed and is missing the moment
when what he believed
didn't go with what he could see,

the few hours just preceding/ordaining
the new instrument,
the new belief.

The gray moving-picture of a shadow-heart that
showed disaster contained, as if not hers
though it was no stranger's.

«*Planck's constant is the quantum of action.*»

The gray moving-picture of her shadow-heart
"as if not hers though it was no stranger's."
And now the physicist dreams

he's slipping out of the lab, barnboard behind the garage,
finding a place in the shed with the other help,
daylight, dim, the fellow escaping companions:

widower engineers
who'd failed a reality too
and now—like him—want a task they can do well.

The glee of the scene
where he's tricked the suspicious man
into offering a *job!*

And then all the long days' job in the room
with a heart, hearing the murmur of singers
behind the two-inch speakers

—Edison, Einstein,
Planck—to attempt
intently—trying—fixiting.

The Sight of Least Regret

After "Moon 3" and "Moon 22,"
by Ann Craven; 1995

The white-clipping moon (3?)
on the left, clear as a night,
is dark where its mass, round,
is clear inside it.

Under the clouds (22)
to the right, the fuller moon
is clear enough, is "unseen," is blurred
light: they're alike, in waiting.

•

The blind never did demand
"pictures"—silent,
furious—but cherished (furious,
silent) the detectable intentions.

The sky's very straight,
Copernicus, Ptolemy—always
geometry: Always
a point! A thin line.

The math as it simply is,
thus learned by heart;
2-plus-8 is a 10,
and that's that.

•

The sun is a line of light
in the black night sky;

a touch at the blind eye now
and the endpoint's warm.

The poles were too far
apart before. Now they are not,
are nearly touching: tactile
black of the clear moon's sky,

or cloud catching blurry
light to the very edge.
I think they were made to be
one—dark, light—separate painting.

•

Home or away upstairs
on a light dark night
like a father waiting to see
before he could die.

*The sky's always straight
in relation to earth*, he meant,
as stars wheeled—*Don't
look up*—in the ocean.

All That Is Symmetric

I was thinking that I wanted symmetry, that
symmetry was possible, desirable, that I could come
to a conclusion and not (nonetheless) leap to conclusions,
as if your death were not after all (death, you) conclusion.

I was thinking in the back yard (snow, smoking)
about what you'd wanted. *If you don't know by now
what I'd want you to write*, says your ignorant moon,
that *ugly chile*, and stops. I was thinking of the mystery

of your *judge that you not be judged*, judging,
and then about our trios together: who'd thought
what when, known different sometime, learned
how to *make the best of it.*

I xeroxed your singular picture for someone else,
not seeing at once how I wanted it for myself.
What the picture was of, I know you'd have been amazed
that I wanted to see it, keep it. One fine day

in the Marina, or along the Embarcadero. A too large cap,
like Spanky's (no, not accurate); your father and mother; coats.
And straight at the camera the face that was you learning,
worried but learning, except with the deep-set eyes

open. I'd never seen it. Now I've kept it. I have been thinking
of you so often, and so often wanting to be so specific.
Too late; too soon. But we were always (young father, daughter,
then older) symmetric.

Only Children

see what the outdoors
world has done.

are indoors, querying even
given the comforting
room of their own.

miss the place at the center
of the receding constellation.

tend to mis-see their things
as animate, animals human,
humans somehow granitic, stone.

Little Sister,

That flag of bright little words you waved
that released passion, or almost
released the passion in our slipped household,

will you remember? An accident,
like a danger. *"Don't go saying those
things like this."* And so his missing it

flowered and spread, a ring of pins
on a ratchet, flywheel oiled and spinning
correctly, bolt sent home and become longing.

Luckily somebody took you aside
and taught you to mistrust passion.

Self-control, he was endlessly saying.
Savings. Don't take the quick way out,
work at the tiny-machinery motors,

missing or stuck keys, stuck then
taken apart, together: the smell of the oil,
the small twanging.

Not just buying
replacement. *"What?"* he says
in the mind's ear:

*"Let's see
if we can't fix it."*

Dear heart, if I failed to grow up
to quench my thirst, or you quenched yours
at birth and you died that soon— Don't worry!

Not everybody can fail like that,
machinery broken, patterning pinned,
ripping in wrath, regathering,

silk slung outward and caught, attempting.
Then engage to mistrust passion,
as he did.

Now that he's died, let's fix things.
Mend them, to mistrust excess.

Students of Grammar

After my father, E. C. Wood (1922–1995)

THE GOLDEN APPLES

The grammar of death is a novel—an epic
novel—and we can't stand to study it much.
All those participial phrases—we don't remember!
—preceding a sentence, like an escape clause.

And "What kind of sentence is *this?*"
they asked us. "Parse it." We'd sweep out
the house, garage, rake out the yard,
to get out of having to parse it,

but still have been pleased to know an *is*
is required with *due to*. Irritated at
"Why *is* it?," we thought we could just not
say, and ignore it, or get by with *because*.

No, we never liked our grammar
but we liked the stories: The dot and the line,
running and/or recumbent. The red orange and
gold apples of peopled paper—we liked

the red of a tale so much, the gold
delicious in gardens, we said the stories alone
could do it, and the grammar killed it.
Although we never took in the rules

of a lesson whenever they taught the rules
as the whole lesson. Oh that grammar
was a bad subject. It could always impale,
and repel, you with a concept.

His Given Name on the Flyleaf

The Elements of Style for hours, a day,
trying to discern his thought train
beyond the pencil markings: "<u>5</u>. Do not
join independent clauses by a comma."

The emphases his own, his own confusion:
"Place a comma before a conjunction
introducing an <u>*independent clause*</u>."
His pencilled capitals: "S E N T E N C E ."

It would have been the language,
the circled "participial" (long-lost
Latin *particeps*, faroff shorthand "partaking"):
"Walking slowly down the road, he saw

a woman accompanied by two children,"
saw a woman with two, not one. *Walking*
an act so allied with its noun or nouns,
simply by placement, it's purely descriptive.

Decide between the ongoing choices of syntax,
the participial jokes ("Page 9" in light-red
pencil): "Being in a dilapidated condition,
I was able to buy the house very cheap,"

"Wondering irresolutely what to do next,
the clock struck twelve." Or the mnemonic
partaking: "He saw a woman, accompanied . . .
walking slowly down the road."

GIVENS

Petites explications de texte, Beginning Greek,
Historia de la lengua española, Latin
Prose Composition. The Elements of Style,
with its question-marked *portcullis.*

The grammatical subject: *"Particeps*
(n.): partaking; confederate, partner,
confidant." And why *aren't* "which"
and "that" both also the same thing?

The same, the greater or lesser, nature
of the connection. Inside the sentence is
or are the partner, confederate, confidant.
Parsing only seeks [him, her, us] out.

The editorial we

Given the Questions

I've begun trying
to tell the truth

whenever I can—
under interrogation.

These great and stripy
red/gold apples—

how could we throw them away?
"The heart of a heartless world

is what's at stake." "Least said,
soonest mended."

No reason whatever
to speak, until we're asked:

On each face
a new construction.

True false bricks.
A mortar of silence,

the telling apple,
gravitation. Apart from this,

the news is bad.
First: How far to go?

Is that too shy,
too all-is-lost?

I am not sure
what all I know.

The one last bridge
is considered crossed

at what point?
How far to go

just now?
These striped-red apples

are *mine* today.
I don't forget

what I have seen. Newton,
the myth, and then these

later ones. Things I had known
are set aside.

We will be punished
too soon. Or so we believe.

We think we know
too much to bear.

Names unnamed,
I'd dare to speak.

Edward M. Stringham
Copied in Pencil

Before when he had the Palmer hand
but better: *palm trees*—light-lined
pencils' curving & flowing, for years,
for thinking remembering-body
Cavafy, self-mnemonic Bacchus or Eos,
Simplicissimus and Orphéo;
for copying out *Zitronen blühn*, lemons
blooming—Goethe envisioning southland;
also for having chosen having chosen.

"It's when he began wearing saffron robes
that I started crossing the street to avoid him,"
saying. Whereas the silvery pencil's continuing
years of reading Russia, birches' vodka,
olivey Greece, Czechoslovakia—*bells, lightness
of being*. He gathered his notes, remembering:
Words & tables & charts—rapt & attentive.
Not rendered out in full, inescapably clear
syntax-solidus-grammar.

His laugh out loud in the world like an outcry
or not; private. Only the end just barely obeyed
a logic, starved for lemon-trees; was not eased.
He was remembering *tiramisù, galaktobouriko*,
ice creams, unworldly candies.
"I've been having existential thoughts," he said:
how to proceed in the world, a worldly place,
ignoring, like dreading not having, money; how
after risking loss to feast on not having being.

To Author Re: Insert

Not to use a single "image"—plain, plain white
like a nothing, and plain cold; not especially harsh
or pressed, strait or distressed; not light
but not so dark, not anywhere near but not far-

distant—would be a good way to do it.
Not to make a cartoon of the deity, mired
in deeper dilemmas, last loss of wit
and volition, as if treading water but tired,

and the stunned dumb opposite of glorified.
Ox hardly splashing; chilled. *Not to be bored*,
the newspapermen used to say: *Why
who what where when?* As if curious: *More.*

In memory Joseph Mitchell (1908–1996)

The Little Bees, Newly Busy

The bees came for their flowered blouses.
    "Oh! Oh! Can't we wear them anyway?"
A visit with coffee, phrases and clauses—
    "Oh *my*. There *is* a lot to say!"
They ate all the cake and *sweet jesus*
    but—uh-oh—were angry anyway.

"All that work and for what? These wages?
    They come anyhow."
"Work in the center, work at the edge, is
    a matter of *luck*—" "No. *Know*how."
Place, peace, and money or times.
    "Not somebody else's whatsit—aegis?"

The bees came for their flowered blouses.
    "Oh, God!" But screens?
The heat in the kitchen almost froze us:
    big flailing—big scene.
"What's *wrong* with these creatures?" "I don't *know*,
    it's whatever they choose to *mean!*"

The New Offices

When they work late

our fellows make up a black-inked hierarchy of beasts. They run
for longer paper, for rulers. They widen the table:

Whether we live under broad green leaves
or under the elms.

Whether we feed in or play in water,
if the water is cold or is warm.

Whether we shed our skin or feathers or fur in the heat
or during a cold night's sleep.

Whether we sleep in the earth—
if so, what color.

How we engender our young, what motion,
and how we feed them.

Right triangles of animal noise, wet from their nighttime pens,
are drying.

Approval, breathed in a wet fog, comes back smelling of
lion, lamb, lark, lizard.

Thin dark windows contain this interior garden, its paper
animals, what we see:

corporal silhouettes taking their explorations through populous
blue to thinned cobalt.

If we are sprung from stone at daylight, at noon, or ever. "All
God's creatures shake hands." A touch added just before dawn.

56

Walk Downhill During
Heat Wave Elsewhere

The right movement of the right foot
on dirt under tree-green grass underfoot,
the right movement of the left foot:

This dance is a dance that is like sex,
a walk downhill—that weirdest aspect.
Gravities erasing force; your grace next,

that side of sex. The cut-grass smell
not yet new hay. The tiny ticks in the grass
gone. Slant-sun grass grass-green

at ten, then under-tree green
at noon— A light, near-kissing wind betweentimes.
Walk in the heat before cool sleep:

a new turn—not some trick-play,
hot, upbraiding the drained streets,
where every step goes dead today.

I hear the city is one big catchphrase: "You'll
pay." As if each misstep would make a fall.
"No care too great, no care too small."

The Lazy Girl Was Never Scolded

Then: New-painted ceilings shed light, in our place,
as if they were living, or holy. That smell was early

spring, with the windows open. Ambition was only
sleeping, or shortly to be awakened, and would not disappear

forever into compliant ambition. One time, I sat down
on the steps of a ladder, holding a cup of black

coffee that nearly woke the world. Paint was spread bright-
yellow into the corners. Turpentine curled

from woodwork and settled. I did not sit straighter.
A willow outside the window reeked in the sun of doing

nothing, up in its branches, its leaves whole stories,
all summer. A long blond girl, dark in the backlight,

I seized what is nowadays made to seem
nearly nothing.

A Walk with an
Abstract Expressionist

1

Only the slightest touch
and the clicketing silver balls
slide into a crack in the floor,
as if they were mercury: Quick.
They're heavy. It slants.
The "beautiful" silver balls
nevertheless.

2

Shattered Braque never made
an analytical portrait
but put round crowns
on a man's hat, curls
on a broken woman: not
black lines alone but
recognizable eyes.

3

The smart brother Picasso had
allowed himself to dismantle
the living girl before,
as if in a visual game,
this part then that,
and when war came
knew how.

4

The desire to think in words
or full sentences again:

A noun, a verb—an object,
as if prepared to
be clear. "Restraint is a
virtue. Repression's
a problem."

5

How hard to use "I" and "you"
to speak of desire!
Better red, a black, a splash
of another effort, the
off-gold. You're right.
You knew the age
and its tenor.

6

Art, of course, displaying reality
once it's been burned. The blue is ash
like a life. What is most
brazen and true is hardest to take.
Now I can turn my back on you
in the museum, agreeing,
in theory.

7

It's only paint like a camera
taking pictures of people
who did not survive misfortune.
As if there were no right thing.
Like you, I've feared and believed
my unconscious
too well.

They Felt It Was Time

It was time to look away from the face,
brush in their right hand. Woman in light of window,
back to shadow, had wanted to say a word.

Man behind her couldn't say much
to the dog half-buried in sand, the white-shirt figure
racing himself, racing and falling.

                                  All turned away
to go fast by and by, and went fast. Glad not having
to see the look on somebody's face:

active genetic landscape glancing—expression
being too painful to see.
Over if loving:

it will end. This you saw in the knife of the tongue,
the woman's desperate lantern. Then:

They painted a black canvas. An unbearable, bright shine.
Three mathematical, shadowed shapes. A perfectly straight line.

The House Style

was only an etiquette, a habit of speech not spoken
but imprinted: half grammar, half manner—salutation
and closing, as if at the end of an evening
a guest at the door were indeed provisioned
for the nightlong siege of information.

Burn marks, say, beside serial commas' courtesy:
1, 2, and 3—for one at a time was shock enough
to register. It was an etiquette invented over time
for a time of disaster, a breath of air
between sorrows. A collection of colliding customs:

a looseleaf of spellings in common—"focussed,"
"vermillion," "coöperation"—with evolving nouns
of place or feeling. Intent could be seen,
so sorrow could be detected, a column of smoke
above a campfire in Genesis, where the law was

only a bivouac. Everything hinged on intentionality:
intentionality governed every step toward a stop
or other outcome. And, just as the editor
in pencil requested "a quiet proof," and down the hall
the faintest of longhands copied the questions clearly

ready for answers ("Is this intentional? . . . Want this?
. . . This what you intended?"), the style itself
was proof—a set of protocols—from when generals themselves
admitted to a need for sustenance, peace, the wartime elixir-
medication. It was assumed there would be an intention.

And so content the attending grammarians attended to style:
the crowd of diaereses, marks of punctuation and emphasis;
details scouting behaviors and landscapes; volition in idiom,
headlines in small capitals—a civil war of distinctions observed
elided. Not a phrenology, though—in truth—almost a religion.

Persons plural

Daily Geography

It was a way of loving our parents,
all the way back to what they said: *Here,*
you look at me when I'm talking.
Long green or brown drives

                        they described.
Changed or unsettled houses. What was wrong
was wrong in a living way. We of course

didn't see it, and dismissed it. I don't see
where they saw any harm in placing things,
every wave on their land got given a new name:
Castle Rock, Pilot Knob—

                        as each ring finger
grew up to wear one ring. While we
see the country different—almost a city, a town:

Pilot Knob, laid under layers of new homes,
Castle Rock only a stone, foundationwork
for only a crossroads, just as New York
lost "York"

                    as soon as its parents spoke it.
I love the moon as a cool white cup
that drops to the tree-claim edge of a farm,

above the string lights left on the ridge of the barn
by strangers. It's one continual sight to see.
Here now, look: see where I'm talking?
As soon as I'm done,

                    we'll think of a name for me.

                              For my cousins

It Is

(1)

a toy bridge—strings and wires—
from here: the proper side
of the river.

Off to the west, approaching,
it's a cathedral.

The sun should go down *beyond*
a river.

That's what it does
when I am at home.

(2)

I've recurringly dreamed the ferry's
crossing the river. I'd fall in,
swim; half-drown.

Be, now and then, lucky—
nearer one shore or another
under an unseen roadway; pull

at the thick water;
breathe again; reach,
fail to go down.

(3)

A thin steel arch to the west is white now:
six-o'clock metal-white sun unpainted.

"But crossing a bridge to the west
leads other places!"

"Crossing a bridge to the east
('Turn quick! black in the sunset!')
will be back home."

(4)

Did I mistake all the rides crossing,
the change of the air—*air*—
in my father and mother's car?

the palisade
gone lower and lower behind us,
blocking the sun,

later light on the hills of houses
before us
just as they are, as versus none.

The grown, swung-cable harp in between
I thought made the oldest sound.

(5)

It is—did I miss it?—all strings
and wires, flight of viscera, essential,
still an invention.

As who say, wartime, "How did you come to feel
so strongly?" or "War! War if you think
our side is the nothing!"

O center alone,
it *is*: even *except* midriver, it is
provincial.

8 P.M., August of This Year

The wet cicadas scree-slide over how many miles
of air surrounding my body? I hear how my ears,

hearing, answer a moment,
ring for a moment,

saying, *Am I blinding myself*
to be in the sun in a summer haze?

No, it's no blind street just now, no
fatal accident. No disaster.

It's not killing myself—just some self-love, some love,
some only pleasure—to be as I am.

The sun's rose neon—brighter. Bright as multiple lumens.
I did avert my eyes to see it.

Rose neon hung to burn on a gray wash. Backwoods here, and all
    around
these noisemakers, ongoing humming creatures.

Here is the sound I've missed
like missing the crows or starlings.

It's just old.
It's a long pleasure:

ongoing humming creatures,
noisemaker-urgent again—

more than halfway loving,
as if it were songs, approaching music.

Is it really only a long pleasure
to be as I am? The scree-slide's swinging around,

but I'm not in danger, not about to be lost in the sun
just yet, or the big sun. The cicadas' round-and-round is

nothing resembling a human quarrel
or losing battle. Is only round.

Detail from the Large Work

The way they bring the camera in
and crop three-quarters off. More: enlarge

the stitches, bringing the single thread
in focus, the stranded intended

margin. Until cloth isn't cloth. Pattern's
a cut line, and no sense in it.

That's how we used to watch a stick
of incense, split into pieces of what

it wasn't: A bright coal first, orange, strange, sufficient.
The uncaught gray. Between them a black band, catching.

And two smoke lines—an eye-trick mixup of funnel edges,
white, low, but rising.

And we would be closeup, close to the little fire,
watching "everything": ashes in warm air,

high, highest, higher.
That's how we missed whole houses burning.

One Thing Alone

He had been the translator of his mother's memories.
She would draw them in a partial language.
Then he would draw them,
and guess the word.

I was leaning on the back porch, facing away from him.
I thought he was exalting one thing alone, but
he was saying where he'd got his skill.
His partialness failed her.

Soon there was no one alive to interpret the word.
To get him to go on, at this point I said,
"It's hard to act so as to be good."
"Good?" he said. "You want to be

good? Tell me you don't want to have all the money on earth."
Forsythia on the windowsill now, here. When I'm alone
and can put people and my failures with them
out of my mind, I'm immensely happy.

Marriages

are not the same—surely you knew that.
Boats, cars without names: a vehicle,
and another vehicle. What something's called
is not its brand name necessarily.

The light world, of being touched then cynical.
The dark world, of being moved then scared.
The speckle-splayed game-bird world
that runs, then flies, between them.

Things speak differently, house to house.
What each house eats is addition
plus subtraction: what a wife brings,
a husband—what food he'll eat,

what she can stand. A pan of chaos
and resolution. Misunderstanding speaks
as a conscious choice—as if—and says
its minuscule reasons. Here he had thought

she would want the yardful of money.
You couldn't guess from the light on the lake,
the latitude, how she in fact found
intolerable, baffling, his working-all-hours

absence. Anyhow: *Sing of the certainties*,
the solid post holding itself to and against the beam,
sturdied by gravity, in post-and-beam construction,
the hopelessly hopeful intention in old-style building.

As They Were

They were always dreaming just the gerund, a whirring
acting-now, ongoing, just beyond acting now
(their dreams might distinguish between *posterity*
and the infinite *eternity*, given if judgment was *last*
or *final*), and yet there was always an infinitive,
a word of being or motion perceived as infinite,
endlessly able, as if to contain
any action among us, plural or singular,
and forever.

Always they were dreaming inside the particular
tin house, dayside tending aluminum—liable
to be dreaming, to plan, like worries' thinking,
the homing home, the reading book, the running race,
but liable (dreaming a perfection coming and acting),
liable to despair or not to despair,
depending. This since, both said, even now
liable takes the infinitive,
as in *to be*.

The Definite Article

was much like the dry-green sea-set Mediterranean island
the princess went to, but longer back, and in a movie
in black-and-white, but sea light, *L'Avventura*,
the name was, the adventure doubly definite, *the man
and the girl, the yacht*—that one—and the, not an island,

or not just any island. The entire point was indirection,
chasing *among the rock formations or boulders, and then
in the town.* Everyone hiding or searching for which,
unable to derive any further clues from the mystery, or else
(late light) almost everyone's fright at all the assuming.

The bejewelled lit people in the grand hotel's lit mirrors!
Not recognizing the others, *the ones walking out, outdoors,
to sit in the darkness.* The definite article
asked me, after I'd asked to be told the truth
—about *the woman? the man? the night spent*

calling and moving, retreating, advancing?
—when I asked for the truth, the definite article
answered, asking but definite, " 'The' truth?"
and instantly repeated, definite, *"The* truth?"

A Solo in I

A geranium set against gray stones shows
how well I live here: on my knees

in showy red light come up to my chin.
As buttercup pollen leaped

to each "Do you?" and I said "Yes,"
like any other girl's my girl skin

shone with it. Then I disliked the answer.
In the Old World, a garden would be

intentional. It would make you rich,
would marry you off, would make you right.

Like my mother. When
I was too young,

I wanted geraniums in that place,
that light, by a stone wall,

and nowhere else. I'd seen them bend
to their lifelong heliotropism, pulled by light,

but grow up straight. With them, I'd thought,
you can count on the answer.

With them, I'd thought, a grown woman
can be rich, and right—can have an answer.

But we were not rich. It was no Old World.
I am not a girl. I am no girl's mother.

On the River Ride at the 25th Reunion

What there was was a spherical rock in sunlight:
the full moon—its light on the strange but known
place to the east—over our side of the river.

I hadn't known at all what the moon meant,
first time round—light in the water
under the bridge back then, sound as a moving barge,

moving silently over the water. "They met
where the river is wide, after a narrows."
This time we left loud music behind,

inside the railing. We could've been speaking of "chemistry"
in idiom, the place where ore changes color in perfect solution.
We saw how our assayed selves could be graded now:

awkward, strangers but precious. Like gold—not just for a moment.
"He heard her saying how the old concepts ('Oh, Chemistry . . .')
had been as weird as a new lesson: incomprehensible but

the pictures more vivid. 'Yes,' he said. 'And I saw Music
different from you. I believed that you guessed
at modes and codas—a second exam!—but missed

how the two were the same. Or, so similar . . .' "
And then we were conscious of it—the odd concept
of chemistry. No longer slaves, but conscious,

able to be brilliant at the one moment only,
as if by surprise. Wanting all to be well—
But we know more now about the insides—eyes, heart,

the small charge that topples the trees of calcium—
of attraction. And instead we embraced
and found a solution in joking, in storytelling.

No need to discern the old needs in the new fellow-passenger,
unproved but proven. And I've changed the story slightly:
to a different scene, a different night—clouds, moon,

stars—seen at a glance in the dark from the lights
of a different ferry, with other loud music. It's a different kind
of insistence, I promise—a longing for non-insistence,

the two protagonists grown
up in the meantime, unproved but still
proven, in this boat neighbors.

Now I Hear It

This weird music we played all the time:
straight statements—country—using the names of the Lord,
a horse, men or women to complain and praise.

I barely remember the sound in the little car,
or how the air blew through between us. Incomprehension
hardly leaves room enough for a true memory.

Accurate sight of the songs out the small window?
What was the Bearswamp Bar, the half night halfway
lost in the woods in the car, but hearing this music.

And what was the week at the beach
later? Drawn back, single-mindedly reading
selfish young Emma, pride and prejudice, and persuasion.

Walking away from the group at the house,
a kitchen of brothers, sisters and large pans,
corn, clams, the colors of lobsters,

all for walks on a dusty side-country road,
inhaling. Trying to think. Bordered by—what?—like
bridalwreath, anarchic bay flowers, wild-rose carnation.

For the Boy Who Was
Also Singing & Listening

1966; misremembrance

The place was land by the river—old
elms, old stone buildings; lawns green,
but still it felt like a camp, a hillocky field,
guardian outpost—I don't know
what it was. The old stone church they
gave us the run of echoed
a nightlong radio, flickering
speech, the places outside.
We'd been having our bluesy music.

Here was the ledge we'd stayed by,
cool and warm to the touch
in the river; woods we came up through,
walking, on a dirt roadway,
not yet kissing,
most of the evenings
listening, one night singing.
How did we manage?

Somebody called it a canon:
the starts, steps, off-kilter—
not just a round, it required attention,
a long half hour of learning *Non nobis*,
foreign syllables, plain
complicated music. Plain music.
Then did the stone of the walls reply,
the way it did in stories:

the way to be like a God
but to be or to keep
what's human—the song in the night
and the baby, love grown up,
death once again. We knew then
that it was glorious. Is this what
we've been fighting over?

Hadn't we seen
how the psalm-note *tuo*
went so high we could
barely reach it? We did
reach it—*o*, our—and
for the long instant
heard us.

The Season

I love so to be in your body
taken up like spring
after a push-push winter fall
through ice.

Wild red sumac in jars, set loose
on a sill since then,
can heal the skin of my backward or
lazy chase,

as I heal your white winter thighs.
I lie in place.
A hundred apologies if somebody's running
step jars me upright.

If my hard black water or snowslide
in corners gets
gathered, hand over handful,
to wash your face.

I do love to be in your body as if it were
spring, when out
of its famous fever what's chilled to the bone
can slide away.

At 43, She Thinks What
to Name Her Children

Oh . . . Firstborn, Asher!—*asher* means "happy"—
because I am happy. Carlyle, Joseph,
Robert and Richard, for family names:
namesakes all unspeakably loved, for all their flaws.

Jean, Margaret, Ila for girls,
to say they were loved, and will be loved.
All of them out of two originals—Margaret Jean,
Ila Margaret—not to be copied.

Or—she hopes, does she?—uncopied by me.
Because not wishing harm on a daughter?
Margaret, Jean, Ila, Margaret—all
speakable now, since now chosen.

Or else—can it be a name for a woman?—
the lastborn, Asher: no, possibly Asher,
"Do what you can—*I love you, Asher,*"
because I'm alone but I am happy.

Sign Language

Where the great hands
spell out the *A*
to *Z* and a
scatter clearly
means *scatter*, a
pinkie held to
the heart then
an eye means
I see, the grammar
of which doesn't
matter: a non-
restrictive
relation's
conveyed by a
gesture; the face
is the only
true place for
expressions of
love, indecision,
rapture; two hands
brushing the
air past the ears
mean "You lost me,"
were over my head,
while love still
appears on the
heart (two crossed hands),
not in the head,
and *practice*
is one hand a plane
planing the back

of the other—
We do so nearly
believe we'll have
said what we needed
to say, with our
long training.

Hark

Watercolor paint on cards

MIDNIGHT BLUE

The midnight blue; the snow sea-green; the blue
spruce in the white blue yard; a window gold

to mean indoors—*show* and *be
shown* makes the decoration. *Wrapped & bowed*

are the wrong words! Deep in the new—
unforeseen—colors in it, inside the seen,

my December is housing itself in darker & lighter paints
and sees a lighted window—peopled—as windows go,

sound nestled in bright gold as if yolk-yellow, to change
obligation: *pleasure*. The deep dark blues

have become only the music, shown. And life I show me
again seen loving, this one month night at least.

Tree with Ornaments by My Mother

It could be a wintering bear this year,
long furred & yet unclassified fat fir, rearing
uncrouched by the couch, a bear cub, my first—
a Douglas?—first ever long-needle pine & name unknown.

So thickly fern-broom-, borzoi-, or yak-feathered,
whisks under eaves, that ornaments disappear:
the forest of branches has made an interior,
all of her ornaments inside in, and not shown.

But let them try to remain hidden! the glass-bird
light paint glows like a house in the woods at four,
snowbound-warm and excited given. It hides this year
but desires to be seen—makes no grief—to be spoken.

This year's tree makes its scent felt across the yards
in between; the past at last has remade the present. *Hark
not to the shining idols* but to their singular deity, inward
invisible bird fir fragrance, who says they could even be broken.

Grace Cathedral Maze

San Francisco, Calif.; 1997

Surely over the centuries somebody wrote
about the Chartres maze?

How just when you think you're getting close
to the center, you're moved away—

as in this re-created medieval joke
made serious—almost—nowadays.

Just thinking that we are close, in that poem,
moves us away.

The Store

A shop like a boat—red tchotchkes!—and look
at the curious community that goes there
curiously.

Alive after the war and the postwar,
passing a pier
and a wall.

Boarding one by one in the rain to respond to
judgment: to look—slow—then waiting inside
to be sure.

Marvelling at shelves of gifts—gifts
but ready for use—and the place
to use them.

A little-window cabinet upstairs on sufferance
at first: blue/white;
wavery windows.

But one day indulged, for
changing, bathing,
for looking out.

Make music, somebody says. *Make music
that can beguile history.*
So many things to *look* at

a long time! And hear: *Accept the gift
whether you deserve it or not.*
Blaze of slippery, bright

paint with wear in the corners, outdoors
a bird like a crow, a dove
in or over the harbor,

and *no one hurt* by the sights,
some even forestalling
harm!

And still an actual place,
with the actual
people.

A riverbank place by a mercury river, later.
"Too pretty to live"—condemned.
But saying, *And when the context—all*

that we can bear to understand
of time and place and a
certain atmosphere, or

history—is blown to bits,
we make what sense we can of what is left.
To leave there having, without having bought.

Remembering the Golden Age

When every comma was a pause for meaning,
inflected speech ran together, a merging of rivers
confluent, and everyone but the slaves understood
the turn of the phrase; everyone caught
the I in the I's of *am staying, am going.*

When mere inflection implied
the *in, to,* over, under—making,
within the bounds of the island
at least, a universal, inflected
language; a heaven of breath
in pasture; a meal, thyme,
at the sacred table—

the hills of the play in the air
in the limestone bowl of the double
theatre, *amphitheatrum*, could even be sung.
And, except for the baffled slaves underneath,
everybody as one knew *pax, antebellum;* peace or pact,
a clearly inflected language, a "universal" comprehension.

Acknowledgments

My thanks to James D. Robinson, the John Simon Guggenheim Memorial Foundation, and the Amy Lowell Poetry Travelling Scholarship Committee, with whose help this book was completed; and to the editors of the following publications, where the poems first appeared:

The Bitter Oleander Review ("Midnight Blue"), *The Boston Review* ("The Definite Article"), *Colorado Review* ("A Myth for the Girl at Bedtime"), *Columbia* ("The Sadness of Not Knowing," "The Secret Note You Were Handed by Lorca"), *The Nation* ("Detail from the Large Work"), *The New Republic* ("All That Is Symmetric," "They Felt It Was Time"), *The New Yorker* ("A Walk with an Abstract Expressionist," "The New Offices" [as "When They Work Late"], "The Season," "The Lazy Girl Was Never Scolded," "Fall Back," "Foolishly Halved, I See You," "Given the Questions," "You've Just Been Told," "Imagine," "One Thing Alone," "The Homeland," "What I Said Afterward" [as "What She . . ."], "Psalm 103 & Vanity," "Marriages," "The Imaginary Picnic," "A Solo in I," "Now I Hear It," "See. See?," "The Store," "8 P.M., August of This Year," "Tree with Ornaments by My Mother," "Sign Language," "Remembering the Golden Age," "Yet Another Categorical Imperative"), *New York Times* ("June Intercedes in the Garden of Roses"), *Open City* ("Almost" [as "A Qualifier of Superlatives"], "The House Style"), *Paris Review* ("The Little Bees, Newly Busy," "Walk Downhill During Heat Wave Elsewhere," "On the River Ride at the 25th Reunion," "Edward M. Stringham Copied in Pencil," "1,985 Years Through a Word Between Us"), *Pivot* ("In Galilea I Listen," "Daily Geography"), *Prairie Schooner* ("At 43, She Thinks What to Name

Her Children"), *Southwest Review* ("A Chance Small Fruit," "For the Boy Who Was Also Singing & Listening"), *The Threepenny Review* ("To Author Re: Insert," "Only Children"), *Yale Review* ("Little Sister,").

Thanks also to Bascove (in whose *Stone and Steel* "It Is" first appeared; Godine) and to Phil Cousineau (for reprinting "June Intercedes in the Garden of Roses," in *Prayers at 3 A.M.;* Harper San Francisco), David Lehman and Star Black ("The House Style," in *The KGB Bar Book of Poems;* Morrow), the Dia Foundation ("A Chance Small Fruit," as a broadside), and Roth Publishing ("The Little Bees, Newly Busy," in *The World's Best Poetry/Poem Finder*).

And, especially, to the Arthur Allens, the Robert J. Herkenratts, and the Gioias, for houseroom and more. And—for almost everything else—to the rest of the Herkenratts, the Macklins, the Reids, and Dwight Allen, Mindy Aloff, Jill Bialosky, Marianne Burke, Vicki and Scott Desjardins, Jimmie Durham, Caroline Fraser, Ed and Becky Robinson French, Mary Stewart Hammond, Orlando J. Hernández, Carol Jerose, Vickie Karp, Michael Lardner, Phillis Levin, Adelaida López Mejía, Mannuccio Mannucci, James McManus, Mary Norris, Colette Purcell, Alison Rose, Clare Rossini, C.L.S., and Arnaldo Sepúlveda.

"Walk, Shepherdess, Walk," the source of several phrases on page 14, was written by Eleanor Farjeon (1881–1965).

The phrase *"Bien morir"* ("To die well"), on page 16, comes from the novel *San Manuel Bueno, Mártir*, by Miguel de Unamuno (1864–1936).

The picture of Federico García Lorca on page 33 is borrowed from Rafael Alberti's "Retornos de un Poeta Asesinado" as translated by Mark Strand ("The Coming Back of an Assassinated Poet," *The Owl's Insomnia: Poems by Rafael Alberti;* Atheneum, 1973).

"Ugly Chile" (page 41) was recorded by George Brunies (1902–1974) in 1943.

The grammatical rules and examples on page 46 are from E. B. White's revision of William Strunk, Jr.,'s *The Elements of Style* (Macmillan, 1959).

"The heart of a heartless world" (page 51) is a phrase of Karl Marx's, referring to religion, in "A Contribution to the Critique of Hegel's 'Philosophy of Law.'"

"The House Style" (pages 62–63) relies extensively on the style book of *The New Yorker*—and also on Eleanor Gould Packard, Ann Goldstein, Lu Burke, Mary Norris, Nancy Holyoke, Elizabeth Pearson-Griffiths, Charles McGrath, John Bennet, Adrienne Foulke, and others who have worked on copy there. The generals are mostly Thomas (Stonewall) Jackson, as described by Ian Frazier in *Family* (1994). "Phrenology" was a pejorative term of Howard Moss's. "A quiet proof" was what William Shawn would write, on a deep-pink "Timely" interoffice routing slip attached to proofs, to Mr. Stringham in the "collating department": "A quiet proof, pls."

The canon *"Non nobis domine, / non nobis, / sed nomine tuo dat gloriam"* (pages 81–82) was composed by William Byrd (1543–1623).

The quotation at the bottom of page 90 is from "In the Realm of Visible Light," a lecture by George W. S. Trow (Whitney Museum, New York; 1987). The quotation at the bottom of page 91 is from an unpublished 1968 essay by Maeve Brennan (1917–1993). Shortly after Robert Kennedy's assassination, she wrote, "It is very hard, sometimes, to make out what people are saying. We must take everything that is said or written in its own context, and when the context—all that we can bear to understand of time and place and a certain atmosphere, or history—is blown to bits, we make what sense we can of what is left."